Original title:
What's the Point of It All? Let's Find Out

Copyright © 2025 Creative Arts Management OÜ
All rights reserved.

Author: Theodore Sinclair
ISBN HARDBACK: 978-1-80566-259-4
ISBN PAPERBACK: 978-1-80566-554-0

Mosaic of Moments

In life's great puzzle, pieces stray,
We search for meaning, every day.
Yet laughter weaves through every seam,
Collecting smiles, like a dream.

A cat wearing socks, oh what a sight,
Chasing a laser, pure delight.
We laugh at the antics, lose track of time,
In moments so silly, we start to rhyme.

Embrace the Enigma

Why do we dance in the pouring rain?
Why eat dessert before the main?
Embrace the quirks, the odd little quirks,
In tangled questions, joy lurks.

A squirrel in a hat, what's he about?
Searching for acorns, without a doubt.
To ponder the silly, my favorite way,
Why not be curious every day?

A Journey Through the Void

Floating through space, it's quite absurd,
We wonder aloud, not a single word.
Stars like confetti, a cosmic affair,
Tickling our brains, with a zany flair.

An alien laughs as we spin and sway,
Offering green snacks, 'Come join our play!'
In this dark void, with laughter and light,
We find our way, falling into delight.

The Compass of Curiosity

With a compass made out of old spoons,
We navigate life, with laughable tunes.
Questions like balloons, they float and twist,
And the answer is hidden in a goofy mist.

Why do we giggle at socks on our feet?
It's the heart of the mystery, oh so sweet!
In every riddle wrapped in a pun,
Let's follow the laughter; it's just begun!

Intersections of Wonder

In a world of whims, we bob and weave,
Chasing squirrels with schemes up our sleeves.
There's a taco joint where dreams collide,
With extra cheese, we take a ride.

A rubber chicken leads us to fate,
With giggles aplenty, it's never too late.
Why dance with shadows when we can be bright?
Let's moonwalk to Mars tonight, alright?

Uncharted Territories of Thought

We sail on boats made of old newspapers,
Sipping soup from mushroom cap wares.
What's the compass? It points to the fridge,
Where leftovers hum a cheesy ridge.

A penguin in a top hat shuffles by,
Twirling like a ballerina in the sky.
We'll check the map, but it's upside down,
As we strut through the streets of Lollipop Town.

The Veil of Mystery

Behind the curtain, there's a mothball dance,
With fuzzy slippers that rarely prance.
Questions fizzle like soda pop,
Bubbles burst, and the answers plop.

A hamster in a cape holds the truth,
With marshmallow clouds for our sleuth.
Round and round, we let thoughts swirl,
In a cotton candy world, let's twirl!

Echoes from the Abyss

Down in the deep where the giggles bounce,
Echoes of laughter do a funny flounce.
Jellyfish serenade the stone-cold rocks,
While the octopus croons in polka dots.

We slip on bananas and simply glide,
In this zany space where fun can't hide.
With a leap and a skip, we chase down the sound,
From depths of silliness, joy is found.

The Labyrinth of Thought

In the maze of my brain,
Thoughts spiral round and round,
Chasing tails and shadows,
Like a dog that won't sit down.

Logic takes a holiday,
While chaos leads the dance,
Jumbled notions waltz away,
Ah, to reason, there's no chance!

Questions linger like a fog,
Trying to find their way,
Like a lost sock in a wash,
They've got all day to play!

Yet in each twist and turn,
Laughter echoes through the halls,
For in this mind's mad circus,
Who really cares after all?

Reflections in the Twilight

At dusk, the thoughts arise,
Like shadows on the street,
They're dancing with the fireflies,
In a world of half-degrees.

Sipping tea from empty cups,
The reflections seem to quip,
"Do you ever feel like this?"
Hands flapping in a script!

Wondering why the stars shine,
Just to tease our sleepy eyes,
Is the moon a giant lamp?
Or just a cosmic surprise?

The humor of existence,
A cosmic joke we share,
So chuckle into the night,
As the universe lays bare.

Seeds of Inquiry

Planting seeds of questions,
In the soil of my mind,
Watered with contemplation,
Funny fruit we hope to find.

The fruits are ripe with laughter,
Tiny giggles take their flight,
"Why do ducks have feathers?"
As I ponder day and night.

Each question sprouts a puzzle,
Like weeds in a garden plot,
Digging deeper into nonsense,
While forgetting what I sought.

But in this silly garden,
Joy blooms in every row,
For the fun's in finding answers,
To questions nobody knows!

The Alchemy of Curiosity

Mixing thoughts like potions,
In a cauldron made of dreams,
Swirling questions in the air,
Like bubbles bursting at the seams.

What if ducks wore top hats?
Or zebras danced with glee?
Transforming nonsense into gold,
As laughter sets us free!

Curiosity's a wizard,
Casting spells of goofy glee,
Turning mundane into magic,
In a wacky jubilee!

So let's stir the pot together,
With our spoons of silly grace,
In this alchemical frenzy,
We'll find joy in every place!

The Quest for the Unfathomable

In a land where questions rain,
And answers hop like frogs on a train,
We ponder why the sky is blue,
And if cats dream of cowboys too.

The squirrel wears a tiny hat,
While pondering the shape of a gnat,
We chase our tales in circles wide,
Like curious kids on a merry ride.

With telescopes made of pasta tubes,
We search for truths in silly cubes,
A noodle monster might hold the key,
If only he'd share his recipe!

In the end, we laugh and cheer,
For every answer is just a sneer,
Yet still we dance, we jump, we twirl,
In the wild and wacky, wondrous swirl.

Constellations of Curiosity

Stars align in patterns strange,
As we seek meaning, try to arrange,
Why do ducks quack in the night?
Could they be planning a flight?

The moon winks with a playful glow,
While jellybeans in rows form a bow,
Questions float like bubbles in air,
What if broccoli wore a pair?

We map our thoughts like stars in space,
Chasing giggles at a frantic pace,
Do ants have dreams of building castles?
Or is that just tales from our fastles?

So gather 'round this cosmic dance,
Where oddities spark a laugh at a glance,
Let's draw a cosmic roadmap bright,
With silliness as our guiding light.

Lines in the Sand of Time

In the grains of sand we carve our fate,
Wondering if turtles animate,
Why does the wind have such a sound?
Could it be hungry, spinning around?

Footprints fill the shore with tales,
Of wayward ships and paper sails,
We chase the waves as they retreat,
Searching for wisdom in every beat.

The sun grins down in golden rays,
As we ponder the meaning of days,
What's life but a dance on the shore?
Footloose and fancy, we'll ask for more.

So laugh with me at the ticking clock,
Join the merry jest of the rock,
In waves of questions, we softly swirl,
In this quirky, sandy, cosmic whirl.

The Searchlight of Insight

With flashlights made of giggles and glee,
We search for truths beneath the tree,
Why do shadows play hide and seek?
Could they have secrets that they sneak?

A paper boat sails on discovery's wave,
While pondering if jellybeans behave,
Do rainbows argue about their hues?
Or swirl around like playful blues?

With magnifying glasses, we peep and pry,
At the zany life of a butterfly,
What's it like to be a flower sprout?
To dance in the breeze and twirl about?

So let's beam brightly into the night,
With humor dressed up in delight,
For every query leads to fun,
In this wild game of what's to come!

The Searchlight's Beam

In a flash, we're caught in a beam,
Chasing thoughts like a comic dream.
Laughter echoes through the night,
Finding joy in every silly plight.

With gusto, we trip on our shoes,
Stumbling into the very worst news.
Yet each misstep paints a grin,
As we dance with the chaos within.

The moon winks, a mischievous host,
As we toast to the quirks we love most.
Life's a joke or so it seems,
We laugh loudly while chasing our dreams.

So here we are, in this wild game,
Chasing beams that never quite tame.
In each giggle, the answer's near,
Embrace the fun and let go of fear.

Unraveling the Tapestry of Existence

Threads of thoughts tangle and weave,
Creating patterns that mislead.
A stitch here, a knot there,
Crafting a life that's wonderfully bare.

In the fabric of everyday hum,
We find joy in the odd and dumb.
Patch it up with laughter and cheer,
Each blunder brings a smile near.

Colorful dreams, some bright, some grey,
Unraveled, yet funny in every way.
A splash of chaos, a dash of delight,
Exploring the absurd in the depth of night.

So let's dance in this woven spree,
With mismatched socks, we're wild and free.
In this tapestry, we play our part,
Finding hilarity in the heart.

Beneath the Surface of Routine

Every morning, the same old song,
Yet underneath, we still belong.
Beneath the grind, the coffee cup,
Lies a spark just waiting to erupt.

Routines march in a funny parade,
Dancing on toes, a comical charade.
Same old faces, same old grind,
Yet hidden gems are what we find.

We laugh at the clock and its sly tick-tock,
It plays a joke as we start to flock.
Routine may seem like a boring plight,
But there's humor behind that daily fight.

So let's stir the pot, shake up the day,
With silly quirks, we'll find our way.
In the mundane, life's joys arise,
Underneath the surface, the fun never lies.

The Paradox of Purpose

Searching for meaning as we play,
Chasing shadows that frolic and sway.
Purpose hides like a clever prank,
Dancing right at the bottom of the tank.

We ponder while standing in line,
Life's great reasons seem so divine.
Yet the greatest truths often come in jest,
Wrapped in laughter, feeling blessed.

Oh, the irony tickles our soul,
As we stumble toward our ultimate goal.
In the question, the answer takes flight,
Purpose revealed with a wink of delight.

So let's embrace the paradox here,
With each giggle, we conquer our fear.
For in the chase lies the sweetest embrace,
As we laugh at our quirks in this curious race.

Reflections in a Broken Mirror

In a shard of glass, I see my grin,
A smile that's cracked, where to begin?
The rubber chicken makes a fine muse,
For all my thoughts, absurd and profuse.

A sock is lost, where did it roam?
In the dryer's grip, it found a home.
The cat thinks it's a game of hide,
While I search for a matching shoe with pride.

A pancake flips, then flies through air,
Why is cooking such a wild affair?
The toaster pops, a battle won,
In kitchen chaos, where's the fun?

It's a dance with fate, I often find,
Life's a riddle, with ties unlined.
So I chuckle at this daily spritz,
In mirth, there lies the ultimate wits.

The Art of Discontent

In the gallery of grumbles, I hang my frown,
Painting over worries, I turn it around.
With spilled paint laughter, I brush the gloom,
In the art of discontent, there's always room.

A statue of me, in a grand pose,
With mismatched socks and a nose that glows.
Critics gather, sipping their tea,
"Is that high art or just plain me?"

A canvas shifts when I take a break,
My brush becomes a fork for cake.
"Is that abstract, or is that me?"
Oh, the joy in finding the beauty to see!

So here's to life, in turbulent hues,
With splashes of joy in the sad reviews.
We're all just artists in a crazy plight,
Making sense of chaos, in the disco light.

Searching for the Golden Thread

In a labyrinth of lint, I spin my tale,
Chasing fluff with vigor, like a little snail.
Digging through cushions for treasure untold,
I seek the golden thread, bright and bold.

The dog steals my sock, in a game of fetch,
"What's the prize?" I shout, and he starts to stretch.
While cats watch smugly from a high shelf,
I question why I can't just sit like them.

A worm crawls by, wearing tiny specs,
It's the wise old sage of what comes next.
"Life's just a yarn," he offers with glee,
"Unravel each moment; it's all free!"

In the quest for meaning, let's not forget,
The fun in the search, no need to fret.
With laughter and whimsy, we dance on this thread,
Finding joy in the journey, it's enough, I said.

The Kaleidoscope of Why

Twisting and turning in a world so wide,
Questions like confetti in a carousel tide.
"Why do birds sing?" asks the curious child,
Nature giggles back, her humor wild.

A pizza spins 'round in my mind like a dream,
Toppings collide like a whimsical scheme.
"Do pepperoni clouds like to float?" I muse,
As sauce drips laughter, giving me clues.

With each twist of fate, colors collide,
Banana peels and joyride side by side.
"Why was the math book so sad?" I sigh,
"Too many problems it couldn't deny!"

In a kaleidoscope world, let's embrace the odd,
Questions are puzzles, an unending facade.
So let's dance in circles, and sing out a why,
For in playful inquiry, we learn to fly.

Dancing with Uncertainty

Twist and twirl in a haze,
Life's a party, full of maze.
Step left, then glide to the right,
Who knows what's hiding in the night?

Socks mismatched, oh what a sight,
Balloons floating, takes to flight.
The music's loud, we laugh and sway,
Inventing reasons every day.

A hop, a skip, let's take a chance,
With every stumble, there's a dance.
Banana peels on the floor, it seems,
Life's just a series of silly dreams.

So grab a friend and spin around,
In whimsy's depths, we've wildly drowned.
With every giggle, doubts take flight,
In this grand show, we're all alright!

The Whispered Questions

In the corner, whispers creep,
'Why's the cat always in the deep?'
Chasing shadows, we test the void,
Seeking answers we once enjoyed.

Why do socks always seem to flee?
Mysterious gaps, no sign you see.
Do cupcakes dream of frosting skies?
With sprinkles falling, can we be wise?

Who knows where the lost keys roam?
In couch cushions, they find a home.
Let's ponder why we trip on air,
While giggling at our silly despair.

Under stars that twinkle bright,
We sip our tea – oh what a sight!
So here's to questions, may they stay,
In laughter's arms, they lead the way!

Tides of Reflection

Waves crash gently, thoughts collide,
In this sea, we try to hide.
Why do jellyfish dance so free?
Do they ponder infinity?

Each ripple brings a brand new glance,
Is life just a series of chance?
Seashells whisper, stories trapped,
Of dreams we've lost and laughter snapped.

Floating boats in a crowded fleet,
Chasing sunsets, oh what a feat!
With every wave, we learn to play,
In this ocean, we drift and sway.

So let the tides lead us far,
To shores unknown, beneath the star.
We'll surf the depths, splashing away,
In the whims of water, let's always stay!

Fragments of a Cosmic Puzzle

Stars scattered like confetti flies,
Do they giggle at our whys?
Building pieces, we search for clues,
In the dark of night, colors fuse.

Puzzles missing, where's the edge?
Perhaps it's fun to make a pledge:
To find the corner, turn it right,
In cosmic quests, we'll burn bright.

Asteroids zooming, in a rush,
Do they wonder, or just hush?
Each twinkling light, a tiny spark,
In the canvas vast, we leave our mark.

So let's embrace this wacky ride,
With each misfit piece, take it in stride.
In laughter and chaos, we find our form,
In the night's embrace, we feel warm.

Cauldron of the Cosmos

In a pot of whims and sparks,
We stir the stars with silly marks.
Galaxies dance like clumsy fools,
As laughter echoes in cosmic schools.

With spoons of dreams, we dip and dive,
Chasing comets, feeling alive.
Each recipe a giggle, a cheer,
In this soup of wonder, never fear.

Aliens chuckle over our plight,
As we fumble through the endless night.
A galaxy served with a side of fries,
Who knew the universe wore such a guise?

So let's sip this broth of time and space,
With a wink and a grin, we embrace the chase.
In the cauldron, we'll find our roles,
Making merry with our jolly souls.

In the Wake of Wandering

On a path paved with zigzag cheer,
We wander aimless, without a fear.
Each step a question, each turn a jest,
Finding humor in our unplanned quest.

Clouds overhead wear goofy hats,
While squirrels mimic our silly chats.
Every stumble turns into a dance,
In this wandering, there's always a chance.

Map in hand, we lose our way,
Trading caution for laughter's sway.
Who needs a destination so grand?
We're explorers in a whimsical land!

So skip along this road of chance,
Embrace the missteps, join the dance.
In wandering, our spirits twirl,
Finding joy in this crazy swirl.

The Mirror of Moments

In a glass that giggles with each glance,
Reflecting lives in a silly dance.
Moments bounce like rubber balls,
As time trips over its own tall walls.

We catch our laughter in each stare,
As memories shuffle with flair.
Each crack is a joke, each gleam a grin,
In this mirror, we see all our kin.

Echoes of laughter from yesteryears,
Tickling thoughts and silly cheers.
Through distorted glass, we find the truth,
That life's a party, filled with youth.

So take a peek, don't ever frown,
This mirror holds both up and down.
In its shine, discover the fun,
Catching moments before they run.

Footprints of Thought

In the sand of ideas, we leave our mark,
Tracing giggles, igniting a spark.
Each footprint a story, a laugh, a muse,
In this beach of pondering, we'll choose.

Waves of wishes wash over the shore,
Tickling toes, asking for more.
As seagulls chuckle at our plight,
We bounce along, hearts alight.

Ideas tumble like tides that flow,
Bringing humor in the ebb and glow.
With every step, we dance our dreams,
Finding joy in the bursts and beams.

So wander this beach of curious thought,
With every footstep, laughter sought.
In this grand adventure, we shall parade,
Footprints of thought never fade.

Paths Woven in Wonder

In a world of twisted trails,
I wear my socks with sandals,
Chasing whimsical tales,
Finding joy in all the scandals.

With every step, a giggle,
As shoes try to outsmart,
But oh, they dance and wiggle,
Wrapped in my carefree heart.

Why fret on paths so straight?
Let's laugh at every turn,
For life's too short to wait,
In every stumble, we learn.

So toss your worries high,
And twirl in the sun's embrace,
Together let us fly,
With joy etched on every face.

The Art of Questioning

Why do ducks quack? Who knows?
Do they ponder the moon's glow?
Can squirrels really wear hats?
And do trees ever get jealous?

Questions bounce like rubber balls,
In a mind that's always whirring,
While the fridge hums and calls,
And my cat keeps on purring.

What color is the wind today?
Does it tickle or does it tease?
Is there a place where thoughts can play,
Or just drift like autumn leaves?

So raise your hand, join the class,
Answering riddles in fits of laughter,
Let each moment pass,
With a smile chasing ever after.

A Map to Nowhere

I've got a map, oh what a joke,
It leads me to the garden shed,
I swear it's made of smoke,
And full of dreams long dead.

X marks the spot, or so they say,
But I found a cat instead,
With a mischievous sway,
It purred like it had the thread.

Turns out the treasure's in the laughs,
Not found in gold or fame,
It's all in silly gaffes,
In life's delightful game.

So toss the maps, embrace the fun,
Let your compass spin and whirl,
For every race that's ever run,
Starts where joy begins to twirl.

Secrets Hidden in Silence

In whispers of the trees at night,
Lies a giggle, soft and bright,
Do leaves gossip? What's their share?
Secrets twirl in the cool night air.

The moon is winking, stars take bets,
On dreams we haven't chance to set,
A silent game, a cosmic prank,
Who knew the cosmos loved to flank?

One sock went missing, lost in the void,
Perhaps it's off on a wild ride,
While I pray the laundry's been enjoyed,
Mysteries wrapped, futility supplied.

Yet in this hush, we find our sound,
With laughter bubbling, joy abound,
In every pause, a story starts,
In silence, we uncover our hearts.

The Maze of Thought

In a tangle of ideas, I roam,
Chasing rabbits toward the unknown.
With each twist, I bump my head,
Wondering why I even fled.

Puzzles dance in a dizzy spree,
Lost in a forest, can't find a tree.
The directions all seem quite wrong,
Yet here I twirl, humming a song.

A squirrel might hold the key, you see,
Though he's munching acorns so carelessly.
I ask him why he seems so wise,
He shrugs and shows me the skies.

In circles, I spiral around my plight,
Searching for answers late at night.
Life's a maze, full of jest,
What's the answer? Is there a quest?

Stories Beneath the Surface

Peeking under the rock I threw,
There's a party of ants, who knew?
They gossip about life's tasty crumbs,
Making me question what really comes.

A snail in a shell, feeling quite grand,
Writes memoirs of travels through the sand.
He waves his tiny flag with cheer,
Saying, 'Behold! The world is near!'

Under the waves, fish spin and giggle,
As bubbles rise, they snicker and wiggle.
Each tale they tell, a slippery chance,
What wisdom lurks in their watery dance?

The deeper I dive, the sillier it seems,
Where logic dissolves in quirky dreams.
Stories unfold with a splashy delight,
What's lurking down there? It's worth a bite!

Navigating the Unknown

A compass spins like a cat on a whim,
While I ponder on a decision so dim.
Maps drawn in crayon cover the ground,
Leading me nowhere, yet quite profound.

With a laugh and a shrug, I take to the air,
Floating along, without a care.
Then a cloud whispers secrets, so sly,
I wonder if it's just passing by.

A signpost asks, 'Left or right?'
I flip a coin, it takes to flight.
What's that? A detour to fun, you say?
I'll follow the breadcrumbs and dance all day!

In the journey of twists, turns indistinct,
I trip over rocks, yet never rethink.
For each stumble, there's laughter, that's true,
What's just ahead? Oh, let's find a clue!

The Heart of Inquiry

A curious heart makes mischief every day,
It questions the sun, the moon, and the play.
Why do ducks quack, and clouds float by?
I gather my courage and aim for the sky.

With magnifying glass, I inspect the odd,
Bugs in a meeting with their tiny God.
Do they deliberate on their next snack?
Or create plans for a little bug hack?

I chase my shadow, he runs away,
Stubbornly refusing to join the fray.
"Why so serious?" I shout with glee,
He laughs, "I reflect your curiosity!"

Exploring the depths of the silly and strange,
Turns the mundane into something to change.
With each question, a chuckle takes flight,
What's missing here? Just a sense of delight!

The Quietude of Wonder

In the silence of a cupcake's glaze,
We ponder life in whimsical ways.
Do fish ever get thirsty too?
Or do they just swim, with no clue?

Balloons float high, like dreams set free,
They giggle and bounce, as happy can be.
If socks have a hole, do they feel sad?
Or do they just dance, feeling not bad?

Lemons laugh when tossed in the air,
Wishing for sunshine, without a care.
Do clouds giggle when they turn grey?
Or just get grumpy, that's their way?

In this quietude, joy we unleash,
With questions absurd, our minds seek peace.
So let's toast to wonder, so quirky and bright,
Life's a grand puzzle, with each silly sight.

The Palette of Possibility

A canvas stretched wide, with colors to play,
Each stroke a thought, in a curious way.
What if rainbows held secrets untold?
Or the sun just smiled because it was bold?

Pigs in hats fly by, oh what a sight!
Twinkling stars giggle, filling the night.
If cheese could dance, what moves would it show?
Would it waltz with the moon or put on a show?

Jellybeans bouncing, with candy-coated dreams,
Exploring the clouds on caramel streams.
What if shadows could chat and would play?
Would they invite us for a bright sunny day?

With a swirl of paint, let our minds race,
In the palette of life, let's find our place.
For every question, a whimsical hue,
In a world full of laughter, let's color anew.

Burning Questions and Gentle Answers

Why does toast always land butter-side down?
Is the moon wearing cheese, like a crown?
Do dreams go on vacation till dawn?
Or do they just party until they're all gone?

A cat with a hat, how dapper is he?
Does he ponder the universe or sip herbal tea?
If ants could sing, what tunes would they croon?
And would they encore under the light of the moon?

Does laughter echo in a hamster's wheel?
Or does it just whirl, not knowing the feel?
If questions are feathers, answers the flight,
Let's soar through the nonsense, embracing delight.

For every odd thought that tickles your brain,
There's a gentle reply, like a soft, warm rain.
Let's wrap up our musings in comfort and cheer,
With each burning question, let's keep it all near.

The Heartbeat of the Universe

A ripple of giggles, like stars in the sky,
Do they wink at the earth as they twinkle by?
If cookies could talk, what stories would flow?
About milk's adventures or the sprinkles' glow?

The trees would chuckle, their branches would sway,
As squirrels in tuxedos put on a display.
Who taught the grass how to dance in the breeze?
Is it the sun, or perhaps bees with ease?

A pancake flipped, what a glorious sight,
Does it nod "thank you" for breakfast delight?
Do shadows giggle when chased by the light?
Or do they just stretch out, feeling polite?

With each heartbeat, the universe hums,
A symphony woven of laughter that drums.
So let's join the rhythm, where joy's never far,
In this dance of existence, we're all shining stars.

Restless Hearts and Silent Minds

In a coffee shop with scattered dreams,
We ponder life's convoluted schemes.
A cat in a hat jumps on the floor,
Is it asking for more or just a door?

Tick-tock goes the clock on the wall,
While we wait for wisdom to call.
A pickle jar shakes; it's feeling bold,
And we wonder if it knows what's gold.

With shoes on our heads, we dance in glee,
A butterfly whispers, 'Just let it be.'
As pie in the sky twirls round and round,
We laugh at the truths that can't be found.

The world's a joke, and we're the jest,
Chasing the answers, we're truly blessed.
With restless hearts we skip and glide,
In silent minds, we take it in stride.

The Pulse of a Questioning Spirit

Bouncing on questions like a rubber ball,
We tumble and fumble, waiting for a call.
A squirrel in the park hosts a debate,
While we speculate on elusive fate.

The moon chuckles down on our plight,
As we search for meaning in the stars so bright.
A banana peel lies, awaiting a quest,
To trip up our thoughts and give them a rest.

With dance moves that leave us quite perplexed,
We spin round in circles, hardly vexed.
Sprinklers spray wisdom, if you get too close,
So we towel off laughter, that's what matters most.

A ticklish breeze nudges at our backs,
Prompting wild thoughts like runaway tracks.
What's next is a puzzle, it seems so clear,
Yet we simply laugh and toss back a cheer.

Whispers in the Silence

In the stillness, the air begins to hum,
As rubber ducks gather for a drum.
We pause for a moment, tiptoe and glance,
At tangled-up thoughts that refuse to dance.

A leaf plays hide and seek with a breeze,
While we chuckle at questions, eager to tease.
The sun winks slyly; shadows do sway,
In the carnival of thoughts, we'll find our way.

With jellybeans swirling in a bowl,
We munch on mischief; it's good for the soul.
Beyond the confusion, there's laughter to find,
In whispers of silence, we loosen the blind.

A clock leaps forward, then backward, too,
Time's a jester, just playing with you.
In the laughter of chaos, we see it all clear,
Life's just a circus, and we're here for the cheer.

The Canvas of Our Becoming

Splashing paint on moments, wild and free,
We weave a tapestry, can't you see?
A dog with a crown joins the parade,
Each splash of color, an unpredictable charade.

Jumping through puddles of glittering thought,
We stumble on wisdom that can't be bought.
With jelly on bread, the world feels right,
As we sketch our stories in this comic flight.

The sun dons a hat; the moon picks a tie,
Confetti of questions flutters up high.
Oh, what a mess, but what fun to explore,
Each brushstroke of laughter opens the door.

As the quirkiness paints our very own dream,
Life's an absurd and delightful scheme.
With every bright hue, we learn to embrace,
That the canvas of life is a whimsical place.

Dancing with Uncertainty

In the garden of questions, we sway,
Tangled in thoughts, bright as a sunray.
With each twist and turn, we all laugh,
Wondering if this is the right path.

The music is odd, a cacophony loud,
Yet we twirl in the chaos, feeling so proud.
Two left feet? Who cares! Let's spin,
Embracing the mess; that's where we begin.

A pirouette of doubts, we don't mind,
In the dance of the clueless, joy is blind.
The floor might be shaky, and so are we,
But isn't that where the fun starts to be?

So come join the frolic, leave worries behind,
In this dance of confusion, we're all intertwined.
Laughing together, we take the leap,
Finding joy in the questions we keep.

Whispers of the Unseen

In the silence of thinking, we hear a hum,
Ideas are floating like bees to the plum.
What's that buzzing? Come closer, don't flee,
It's probably nonsense, just like you and me.

A shadowy figure, a ghost of a thought,
Tickles your mind with the answers it's brought.
But just as you reach it, it flits out of sight,
Leaving you laughing alone in the night.

We ponder in riddles, sincerity blurred,
Searching for meanings, absurdly unheard.
But oh, what a circus, this journey so wild,
Every twist of the mind makes you feel like a child.

Embrace the unseen, it's witty and grand,
In the theater of life, we're all in demand.
With whispers of wisdom shared over tea,
Let's toast to the chaos of you and me!

Chasing Shadows of Significance

Running in circles, we scream at the sky,
Where are the answers? Oh me, oh my!
With nets made of humor, we catch every whim,
Dancing in shadows, it's a laugh to the brim.

The meaning is hiding, or so it would seem,
Yet chasing these shadows is the heart of the dream.
Often confused, but always in motion,
Laughter erupts like a quirky ocean.

Through fields of absurdity, we sprint with delight,
Chasing shiny signs that fade from our sight.
Were those question marks, or just wavy lines?
In this playful pursuit, our joy intertwines.

So let's keep on running, on this silly quest,
Finding humor in pondering, it's truly the best.
For in every last doubt that gets tossed to and fro,
We discover the fun of the not-knowing glow.

The Longing for Clarity

On a quest for a lighthouse, we sail in the mist,
With maps full of giggles, we don't want to resist.
What is the compass? Where do we point?
Let's laugh at the riddle, oh what a joint!

Foggy conditions, absurdly unclear,
But we giggle and shrug; there's nothing to fear.
With each wave of confusion, we cheer and we sing,
For clarity's overrated—let's make this our thing!

We fish for wisdom in a piñata of dreams,
Hoping for fortune but pulling at seams.
Yet in every small failure, we splash in delight,
Finding joy in the chaos is perfectly right.

So let's sail along with our whimsical crew,
In the sea of uncertainty, we'll find something new.
With laughter our anchor, our goal's crystal clear,
It's not about answers, but the fun we hold dear.

Ripples in a Still Pond

A pebble skips across the lake,
Causing splashes, make no mistake!
Fish applaud with a giddy grin,
"Now that's a dance, let's do it again!"

The old frog croaks, he takes a leap,
"This pond's not so dull, it's ours to keep!"
Turtles nod, in their casual way,
"We'll ponder life but hey, let's play!"

Sunbeams bounce from stone to stone,
The water shimmers, feeling at home.
"Why swim in circles?" asks a newt,
"It's more fun to chase a loose boot!"

So round they go, in their froggy boots,
Creating laughter in muddy roots.
Who knew such joy could be a thing,
And laughter makes the pondbirds sing!

The Beauty of the Unanswered.

Questions bloom like daisies in the field,
With answers tangled, never revealed.
The sun winks, "Just enjoy the show!"
While bees buzz by with a cheery "Hello!"

The clouds gather, they whisper and tease,
"Life's much more fun with a bit of unease!"
Grasshoppers hop, their dreams take flight,
"Let's question the stars under the moonlight!"

In a patch of daisies, a ladybug spins,
"What's better: the chase or the wins?"
A butterfly giggles, flutters away,
"Who cares about answers? Just love the play!"

So round and round the pondering goes,
In the beauty of chaos, nobody knows.
With every twist in this crazy dance,
We share a smile at the silly chance!

The Quest for Meaning's Tide

A crab scuttles sideways, looking for gold,
A treasure map written but never told.
"Why dig for meaning in the sand?"
The waves just laugh, "Take life in hand!"

The seagulls squawk, with nothing to say,
"Find your fortune while you play!"
They swoop and dive, without a care,
"How much fun is chasing the air?"

Dunes shift and sway, a dance so grand,
Leading all critters to make a band.
The tides pull in, with a giggly roar,
"Who needs meaning? Let's dance on the shore!"

So we build our castles, tall and bright,
As the ocean whispers in the fading light.
With each wave's crash, we all agree,
Life's a joke, as funny as can be!

In Search of Clarity

A hamster runs fast on a wheel with glee,
Chasing shadows, so wild and free.
"What's clear?" he wonders, with a twist and turn,
As the world outside continues to churn.

Goldfish swims circles in his dazzling bowl,
"Do I need clarity? Or just a stroll?"
With bubbles rising, he quips to a friend,
"Let's not be serious, let's just pretend!"

The wise old owl, perched high on a beam,
Says, "Search for wisdom but keep it a dream!"
With a flap of his wings and a chuckle so bold,
"Life's less of a puzzle when it's made of gold!"

So join the dance, take a step or two,
In the riddle of fun, clarity's for you.
Embrace the sillies, the joy on the way,
For life's a laugh on this wonder-filled play!

Questing in the Quiet

In shadows soft, we wander slow,
Our laughter echoes, a gentle flow.
With squirrels as our guides, we chase,
Every nutty riddle, a funny race.

A leaf falls down, a secret shared,
Why is the sky blue? We both declared.
Chasing the clouds, with silly glee,
Who knew questions could be so free?

We stumbled on dreams, on paths less trod,
In the quest for answers, we nod and prod.
With each little giggle, our wisdom grows,
Navigating nonsense, as everybody knows.

Unraveling thoughts like a tangled thread,
In our quiet quest, ahead lies Fred.
He's got the answers, or maybe a sock,
Join us in laughter, we'll dance 'round the clock.

Circles of Inquiry

Round and round, we spin the wheel,
What's true or not? It's hard to feel.
With hats made of questions, we prance and sway,
Who needs direction anyway?

Why do zebras have stripes, oh dear?
Together we ponder, while sipping beer.
Each sip is a question, each laugh a clue,
In our circle game, it's me and you.

Logic is lost in the whirl of fun,
With giggling theories, we'll never be done.
Why does the sun rise, or does it fall?
In these circles of thought, we giggle and crawl.

The truth is a puzzle, or perhaps a prank,
With questions like fish, we swim in a tank.
So let's keep exploring, with hearts full of glee,
In circles of inquiry, you're stuck with me!

Refracted Realities

A prism of thoughts, all twisted and bright,
Bending our minds with kaleidoscope light.
Why is a cat not a silly old shoe?
In refracted realities, anything's true!

Twist and shout, let's break the mold,
With wacky ideas, and stories retold.
Do fish wear pajamas when they swim at night?
In our world of logic, there's no need for fright.

Each view is a giggle, a silly surprise,
With reality bending, we open our eyes.
What if squirrels are plotting a scheme?
In refracted visions, we burst into dream.

With laughter as fuel, we'll shine like a star,
Chasing reflections, no matter how far.
So let's keep refracting our curious minds,
In this wacky reality, new magic we'll find!

The Labyrinth of Existence

In a maze of life, where questions roam,
With twists and turns, it feels like home.
Why does the sky wear a fuzzy shawl?
In this labyrinth, we giggle and sprawl.

Each corner we turn, a riddle awaits,
With the signs all jumbled, we play with fate.
A Minotaur? Nah, just a dog with a bone,
Chasing shadows, our laughter is grown.

With maps made of whimsy, we doodle and dart,
These mazes of nonsense are works of art.
Who needs the answers when questions are fun?
In this labyrinth of life, we run and we run.

So grab a good friend, let's lose track of time,
In this twisty abode, life's a whimsical rhyme.
With each step we take, we dance and we play,
In the labyrinth of existence, let's play all day!

The Questing Heart

In search of joy, we roam the land,
With maps that lead to ice cream stands.
We chase our dreams like squirrels chase nuts,
While tripping over our own silly butts.

With laughter echoing through the park,
We wonder if we've missed the mark.
Yet every slip and fall, we see,
A chance to giggle, wild and free.

We scribble plans on napkins bright,
While sandwich crumbs take off in flight.
The universe may roll its eyes,
But who needs sense when fun's the prize?

Through life's maze, we bounce and bounce,
With every twist, we read the pounce.
So here we dance with glee, oh yes!
To seek the great, absurd success!

Threads of Ambiguity

We weave our tales with colors bold,
Yet caution whispers, 'What's the hold?'
Like knitting sweaters for a cat,
We wonder if it's worth the spat.

In tangled yarns of life we play,
With socks mismatched, we find our way.
A patchwork quilt of good and odd,
Presents the truth that we applaud.

In deep discussions, fluffed with air,
We philosophize while in our chair.
The meaning's found in dreams we chase,
As giggles paint our cosmic space.

So come, let's dance in chaos sweet,
With laughter wrapped around our feet.
For in this maze of twists and bends,
The joy we seek, it never ends!

Embracing Life's Mysteries

We hold our questions like a kite,
Letting them soar, oh what a sight!
In fields of whimsy, we frolic around,
Finding laughter where answers abound.

The squirrels quiz us with beady eyes,
As we climb trees and reach for skies.
In every riddle, a lesson grows,
Like spaghetti that twists and flows.

With fortune cookies, we break the seal,
What do they say? Oh, quite surreal!
Yet if we snack, and don't just ponder,
We'll find the magic we all wander.

So let's embrace our puzzled fates,
With every stumble, life creates.
For mystery's charm is truly bright,
In giggles and glee, we find our light!

The Echoes of Our Choices

Like echoes bouncing off the walls,
Our choices ring through laughter's halls.
We toss confetti with every bet,
While searching for a safety net.

With sandwiches held in whimsical sway,
We ponder if it's 'eat' or 'play.'
Our whims decide our lunch today,
In fits of glee, we've lost the way.

The paths we take are filled with glee,
Where every choice coaxes a "Whee!"
With jellybeans and silly hats,
We find the joy amidst the spats.

Our laughter follows like a light,
Guiding us boldly into the night.
In echoes sweet, we hear our voice,
For in the chaos, we rejoice!

Dreamscapes of Discovery

In a world where socks disappear,
Chasing dreams without any fear.
Will we find that missing mate,
   Or is it just a sock's fate?

With every quest, we lose our shoes,
Dodging questions we can't refuse.
The universe plans a funny twist,
  Perhaps it's not so bad to miss!

In gardens where the gnomes all dance,
We stumble through a silly trance.
Could this be the meaning we seek?
Or just a joke from some mystique?

So let's embrace the unseen trails,
With laughter echoing in our sails.
For what if life's a game to play?
Let's roll the dice and laugh away!

The Allure of the Unfathomable

Beneath the waves, where fish wear hats,
A party starts with clumsy chats.
Do whales compose symphonic tunes,
Or is it just a moonlit ruse?

In space, where aliens might groove,
Do they find joy in funky moves?
With glowing stars as their disco lights,
They dance and spin through endless nights.

But here on Earth, we scratch our heads,
Finding depth beneath our beds.
The crumbs of snacks, a trail we leave,
What lessons do these crumbs perceive?

Maybe answers lie in laughter's reach,
Or wisdom spun like a silly speech.
So, let's dive into the absurd,
To find the joy in every word!

Illuminations in the Dark

In shadows lurk the playful lights,
They flicker on, then take to flights.
Are they wise or just a tease?
A joke we laugh at on our knees?

The moon winks down, a cheeky friend,
Promising fun 'til the night's end.
We search for glow in the quirkiest sights,
Like raccoons dressed in shining tights.

With lanterns made from pickle jars,
We stumble 'round beneath the stars.
Is it wisdom that we seek to find,
Or just a place to unwind our minds?

The answers hide in silly games,
Where each misstep provides new claims.
So let's light up our curious spark,
And dance with joy inside the dark!

The Puzzle of Everyday Wonders

A puzzle sits upon the floor,
Pieces scattered, can't find the core.
In kitchens filled with flour dust,
We wonder if it's all a must.

With toast that lands upon its edge,
A talent that breaks all wehedge.
Can burnt offerings teach us grace,
While we giggle in this space?

The cat's concern with yarn's long trail,
Or squirrels plotting with nuts to scale.
What clever schemes are going down?
Perhaps treasure lurks in our old town?

So let's embrace the silly hues,
The puzzle's charm and tomfoolery cues.
For in the quirks of life's grand plan,
We may find purpose, yes we can!

Unfolding the Layers of Life

Peeling back the onion skin,
What's underneath? Let's begin!
A sock with holes, a missing shoe,
Life's a puzzle, who knew?

Juggling dreams like rubber ducks,
In a pond of silly luck.
Each splash a giggle, each gasp a cheer,
Oh, the joy of living here!

Underneath that frown, a grin,
Let's dance around, the laughter spins.
Who needs a map when joy's the guide?
Let's ride this wacky, wild tide!

So bring your quirks, and quirky pals,
We'll monkey around and have a ball.
Together let's embrace the fun,
In this game of life, we've already won!

Trails of the Unsung

Hiking trails with mismatched shoes,
Forgotten paths, with silly views.
A squirrel steals my sandwich right away,
Life's comedy in full display!

With flowers dancing in the breeze,
And bees that hum with such great ease,
A tale unfolds, ridiculous yet real,
Each step a laugh, each turn a reel.

Lost my hat upon a tree,
It waved goodbye, quite cheekily.
As I chase my headgear's flight,
Life composes its own delight.

So let's march on, you and I,
Chasing dreams that might just fly.
In trails unseen, let's take a chance,
With laughter's song, we'll giggle and dance!

Sketches of the Soul's Journey

Sketching life with crayon dreams,
Colors spilled like sunlit beams.
A wild doodle on the fridge,
My heart's an artist on the edge!

Oh, the canvas, a bit askew,
Paint splatters that say "I love you!"
With laughter lines and silly hues,
Life's gallery, filled with clues.

A puppet show of ups and downs,
With giggles echoing through the towns.
Let's paint this path, however odd,
In strokes of joy, we'll take a nod.

So let's sketch more, and laugh along,
Creating tunes, a silly song.
In our vibrant, messy art,
Life's a masterpiece that we impart!

The Odyssey of Introspection

Sailing forth on thoughts that float,
A rubber duck, my trusty boat.
Waves of giggles toss me high,
Why not sail? Just give it a try!

Navigating through the sea of glee,
With pirates' hats and cups of tea.
If introspection's such a chore,
Why not laugh a little more?

Stories told with silly flares,
A treasure map of laughs and cares.
With every twist, a joke unfolds,
A comedy of truths untold.

So hoist the sails, let's find our way,
In this voyage, come what may.
With laughter in our hearts, we'll dare,
To dive deep into this funny air!

Echoes of a Wandering Mind

In a world where socks go missing,
Questions dance with glee,
Chasing thoughts that playfully tease,
Lives like puzzles, wild and free.

Lost keys hide in the sofa depths,
While cats plot a grand escape,
Life's an endless scavenger hunt,
With mischief woven in every cape.

Bouncing thoughts like rubber balls,
Colliding loud with dreams gone awry,
Wandering minds in humor's grip,
Seeking joy in the nearby pie.

So let's embrace the chaos near,
As laughter echoes through our day,
For life's a game of silly chance,
And we're the players in this play.

The Fabric of Purpose

Thread by thread, we stitch our fate,
With mismatched patches, bold and bright,
Some days are quiet, others loud,
A quirky quilt beneath starlight.

Why do we wear our thoughts so plain?
When polka dots would bring us cheer?
Sailing boats on coffee cups,
Each sip a laugh, each grin sincere.

Weaving tales of whimsical dreams,
With a dash of silly serendipity,
Tangled yarns and knotted plans,
Finding joy in absurdity.

So grab your needles, dance along,
Create your fabric, loud and true,
For in this patchwork of the day,
Purpose winks from every hue.

Where Shadows Meet Light

In the corners where laughter hides,
Shadows play a cheeky game,
They whisper jokes to the bright sun,
Inviting light to join in fame.

Bouncing beams with playful grins,
Chasing shadows through the trees,
If darkness had a sense of fun,
It would dance along with ease.

Why ponder deep in endless nights?
When witticisms are just nearby,
With every flicker, shadows tease,
As if to say, "Don't be so shy!"

The dance of light and dark we share,
Unfolds the joy in sweet surprise,
For where the shadows meet the light,
Laughter sparkles in our eyes.

Unraveled Threads of Existence

An endless spool of rambled thoughts,
Twisting tales in colors bright,
Some knot up tight, while others fray,
Yet all are woven with delight.

Why seek the meaning in straight lines?
When spirals tickle in delight,
Life unwinds in joyous loops,
As we twirl through the day and night.

A tapestry of whimsy spun,
With laughter stitched in every seam,
Unraveling threads, we find our way,
In the madness of a dreamer's dream.

So let each quirk and twist amaze,
For every thread's a chance to play,
And in this fabric, rich and bold,
Existence dances, come what may.

Beyond the Veil of the Mundane

In a world of socks and lost keys,
We ponder the mysteries of busy bees.
Are they buzzing for fun or making a plan?
Should we follow their lead, or just stick to the can?

The cat in the window just gives us a stare,
As if she knows truths that are floating in air.
Is life just a puzzle, or is that a myth?
Should we chase every butterfly, or stay at our fifth?

With cereal soirées and fridge magnets stuck,
We wonder if fortune could really just duck.
Do the goldfish in bowls hold the secrets of fate?
Or are they just swimming, saying, "Not today, mate?"

Under the veil of our daily routine,
Do we dance to the chaos or just land in between?
With giggles and chuckles, life's not uniform,
Let's embrace all the quirks; they might just be the norm.

A Symphony of Doubts

Every morning we question, 'What's on the agenda?'
The coffee's too weak, and the toast is a blender.
Do we need a grand plan, or just go with the flow?
Maybe life's just a show, with everyone in tow.

Is the traffic a sign of a cosmic mistake?
Or just earth's way of saying, 'For goodness' sake!'
With GPS voices that can't find their own way,
Do we trust in the journey or just pray for a ray?

With forks in the road and choices galore,
We stumble in confusion while looking for more.
Each laugh and each sigh, it's a curious blend,
Is the journey the point, or just time to transcend?

In this quirky symphony of doubt and delight,
Shall we dance to the beat of the day and the night?
Let's twirl with each whim and each bizarre twist,
For the fun is in finding the paths we have missed.

Starlight on an Empty Canvas

With a sprinkle of stars on a blank piece of space,
We doodle our dreams, though they're hard to trace.
Is the universe laughing, or is it just me?
Creating constellations that are hard to foresee?

Brush in hand, I throw colors with flair,
Maybe life's just a canvas, and we're the air.
Do llamas in pajamas ponder life's twist?
Or are they just munching on grass, too blissed?

Gazing up at the heavens, we search for a clue,
Is the meaning of life in a song with no tune?
Do we paint with emotions or scribble with glee?
Shall we dance in the starlight, just carefree?

So let's splash our desires on this grand, empty space,
Wandering artists in a jubilant race.
With each stroke and smile, let's create as we go,
In the starlight we find that the journey is glow!

Fragments of a Fading Dream

Once I dreamt of a world where socks were a gold,
Where jellybeans grew on trees, or so I was told.
Now reality whispers, 'Hey, wake up, my friend!'
But do dreams really fade, or just take a new bend?

In fragments of laughter and moments we chase,
Do the giggles we gather just light up our space?
Is the cake that we bake a mirage in the mist?
Or is it a reminder that dreams can insist?

As we wander this maze with our quirky attire,
Every blunder a note in our offbeat choir.
Do we hold onto visions, or invent new themes?
Let's stitch all the nonsense right into our dreams!

Underneath our fantasies lies a riddle most true,
Is the dance that we choose really shaping our view?
With each chuckle, each slip, let's celebrate all,
For the laughter persists, like a grand carnival!

The Quest for Meaning

In the garden of thought, I planted a seed,
Hoping for wisdom, or at least a good feed.
A squirrel stopped by, he offered a snack,
Now I'm pondering cheese, instead of the track.

With magnifying glass, I scanned the ground,
Searching for answers, but lizards abound.
They laugh and they play; they seem so content,
While I'm here alarmed, by my time poorly spent.

I asked a wise owl, perched high in a tree,
"Do you know the meaning?" He laughed with glee.
"Life's a strange puzzle, with pieces all round,
But the pieces like pizza, you won't hear a sound!"

So I dance in the mud, where absurdness is king,
Maybe the laughs are the point of this fling.
With a hop and a skip, I've finally found,
The joy of this quest, in the silliness abound.

Digging for Diamonds in the Mud

With a shovel so bright, I started to dig,
In the muck and the mire, I thought I'd be big.
Looking for treasures, all shiny and new,
But found only worms who said, "Good day to you!"

I asked a fat frog, "Do you know where they are?"
He croaked and he splashed, "Not in this bizarre!"
But I kept on tunneling, hopes tied to a charm,
Annoying the bugs, who thought me quite warm.

"Oh look," squeaked a mouse, "You've found the lost shoe!
It's a treasure, you know, if you're into the goo!"
With a grin and a laugh, I declared with bold flair,
At least I dug deep, and don't really care!

In this quest for bling, I found joy in the grime,
Turning mud into laughter; now that's really prime.
So here's to the search, wherever it goes,
The greatest find's laughter, as everybody knows.

Echoes of the Infinite

In the hall of reflections, I shouted real loud,
"Hey, is anybody there?" to the echoing crowd.
Back came a giggle, "Oh yes, it's just me!
But I'm busy reflecting on my next cup of tea."

I wandered the halls, playing tag with no one,
As my thoughts bounced around like a ball in the sun.
"Is this all there is?" I questioned the walls,
They whispered, "Keep asking, it's all that's your call."

In this funny old maze, ideas took flight,
Like a chicken who danced through the stillness of night.
"Cluck-cluck," said the walls, "And never forget,
The quest for the answers is a dance with regret!"

So I twirled and I swayed, lost in the fun,
Chasing shadows and laughter; oh what have I spun?
The echoes keep coming, like jokes from the void,
The laughter, not answers, is what I enjoyed.

Wandering Through the Why

I strolled through the garden, confused by the plot,
Wondering why it is, I'm questioning a lot.
"Hey sunflower!" I yelled, "What's the meaning of this?"

"It's just to be pretty," it replied with a hiss.

I spotted a tulip, all dressed up in style,
"Share your wisdom, friend, even just for a while."
With a twirl in the breeze, it simply replied,
"Sometimes you bloom, and sometimes you hide."

A bee buzzed on by, with a wink and a hum,
"Life's honey in search; it's a pie with no crumb!"
I scratched my head, feeling lost in the whirl,
The flowers are wise; they just dance and twirl.

So I laughed at the journey, each question I bore,
With giggles and grins, who could want anything more?
While wandering through why, peace whispered aloud,
"Just play in the garden, don't worry, be proud!"

Shadows of a Thoughtful Heart

In shadows deep, where giggles reside,
A pondering mind took a whimsical ride.
Chasing dreams and bright banana peels,
Danced with laughter, skipping life's reels.

What is the reason for a pie in the sky?
Perhaps it's for sharing, oh my, oh my!
With whipped cream wishes and sprinkles of cheer,
Delightfully dizzy, we linger here.

So let's flip the script and juggle our woes,
For every sad thought, a tickle that grows.
In the circus of life, we skip and we sway,
Painted with humor, we frolic all day.

Yet in the maze of our curious quest,
We find the absurdity, smiles manifest.
So here's to the whimsy and shadows we chase,
In giggle-filled moments, we find our true place.

The Language of Lost Moments

In a world of whispers, time spills like tea,
Laughter escapes as we spill our glee.
Every missed chance, a poke in the side,
With each quirky glance, we giggle and glide.

Now what's that tune we sang in our teens?
Was it crooning or clashing? Sweet memories glean.
With dances of dust bunnies, swirling around,
The language of chaos, hilariously found.

As we gather the moments we carelessly saved,
Life's a buffet, and we're wildly paved.
Silly old habits like dressing in stripes,
Turn the mundane into quirky delights.

So gather your giggles and treasure the jest,
In lost little moments, let humor invest.
For life's greatest questions unfold in delight,
As we trip through the laughter, our hearts feel so light.

Epiphanies in the Ether

A puff of confusion, a tickle of light,
Epiphanies bloom in the soft shimm'ring night.
With socks that don't match and hair that's askew,
Wisdom sits giggling, just waiting for you.

In the whirl of our musings, a chuckle might land,
While pondering fish that can tango on sand.
We cogitate boldly on what won't eat lunch,
Finding treasure in nonsense — a radiant hunch.

With questions like marbles, we roll them with glee,
What if the universe craves peanut butter tea?
So let's sashay boldly to flavors unknown,
Where laughter's the key, and the seeds can be sown.

Venturing further, we swoop through the air,
High-fiving the blunders, without a care.
Through laughter and quirks, our spirits we'll lift,
In a realm where absurdity's the greatest gift.

Searching for the Soul's Map

With a map made of giggles and compass of fun,
We scour the universe, all questions as one.
Where is the soul? Oh, let's take a peek,
In quirks and in chuckles, the answers may speak.

Through valleys of puzzlement, rivers of jest,
We navigate nonsense, poised for the quest.
In riddles and rhymes, like clouds drawn in air,
The soul's true location? It's everywhere!

With every misstep, a dance we create,
Twists and turns lead to the joy we await.
For in searching for purpose, let's revel in play,
Stitching threads of laughter throughout the way.

So here's to our journey, let's frolic and roam,
Discovering truth in each giggle and poem.
For the map of our souls is a tapestry bright,
Woven with humor, our guiding light.

Light Cast on the Unknown

In shadows where the giggles hide,
We search for truths that coincide.
But every fact's a wobbly friend,
And who knows where this nonsense ends?

A cat walks by with secret glee,
Proclaiming all it wants to be.
With every leap, it questions fate,
As if we're wise—or just first-rate.

Our bouncing thoughts like ping-pong balls,
They dance around, but never call.
We laugh aloud at every guess,
Finding fun in the absurd mess.

So let's embrace this wild charade,
In laughter's arms, we're serenade.
Perhaps the quests are all for kicks,
As joy's the answer—make it quick!

Dreams that Flicker and Fade

I had a dream the other night,
Where socks could talk and roast the light.
They giggled loud at my old shoes,
Claiming I've got fashion flues!

A hovercat swept through my thoughts,
With theories wilder than my socks.
It whispered softly, 'Chase the whim,
For life's too silly to be grim.'

But in the morning, all was gone,
Just memories of sock-worn dawn.
Though dreams may flicker, fade, and flee,
The laughter stays—and sets us free!

So here's a nod to dreams we chase,
For in our hearts, they find their place.
Though wacky paths, we stroll with cheer,
Tomorrow's riddle's waiting here!

Chronicles of the Unseen

In pages blank, where scribbles play,
A tale spins round in disarray.
Invisible ink tells secrets bold,
Of creatures lost, and treasures told.

A rubber duck in viking hats,
And dogs who run with fancy cats.
They frolic through these tales we weave,
Inviting us to laugh and believe.

With every sentence, laughter grows,
Wouldn't you know? The plot just goes!
We scribble laughs, and wince at fears,
As unseen jokers spill their cheers.

So dive into this merry spree,
Where chronicles of joy run free.
The unseen shines where giggles dwell,
In playful prose, we find our spell!

The Unspeakable Search

In quest for things that slip away,
We ponder what they might say.
A dinosaur might boast a rhyme,
Or colored socks that dance through time.

A searcher trips on cosmic pies,
And winks at aliens in disguise.
Together they will mock the chase,
For truths can wear a silly face.

We giggle at the unspeakable,
As questions float, quite peekable.
What's hiding in this laughing maze?
Perhaps the fun's the only praise!

So let's embark with quirky zest,
In chasing laughs, we'll find our quest.
For every riddle brings delight,
In this absurd, enchanting night!

www.ingramcontent.com/pod-product-compliance
Lightning Source LLC
Chambersburg PA
CBHW051635160426
43209CB00004B/654